The Sea Inside

John Brice

The Sea Inside
Published through IngramSpark

ISBN: 979-8-3507-0480-8

Beginning.

More than twenty years have come and
gone and now I am ready to share.
The sea has always called to me. I believe we each have
one inside of us. I hope you enjoy the view into this one.

This book is dedicated with thanks to,

Carolina
Ollie
Jackson
Isla
Maeve

Contents

Remembering Youth

Adults are just children that have done some living.

"And now here is my secret, a very simple secret: It
is only with the heart that one can see rightly; what
is essential is invisible to the eye." (The Fox)
—*The Little Prince*, Antoine de Saint-Exupery

A gardener's song

(Plum Island, 2014)

When I moved dirt and sweat was my reward,

and an ache, but one that reminded me
of things moved, came after;

when things were done, and real and true,

and had felt sun on the skin, and my hair was thick and free,

and my arms were strong and full,

and my hands were rough and marked,

with the sign of my work;

and when paused the wind would cool me,

and my thoughts were on only how to
straighten the old stone wall,

laid out in a sloping welcomed challenge before me,

those days, in between the spring mud
and when all the leaves had left,

my fruitful world.

Kezar Lake

(St. Simons Island, 2022)

It was the purest kind of still,
When the dawn was rising,
And the cold air drifted over the blue-grey lake,
Surrounded by thick firs crowding the shores,
Hidden inlets,
The loons sitting quietly.
I would slip off the u-shaped dock into the deep,
Unable to see my feet,
And a rush came to my insides when I submerged,
Silver canoes stacked sideways,
The big rock that only dipped its bottom into the shallow end,
And the green clapboard of the boathouse were my companions.
This was the full freedom of youth,
My early morning ritual,
Beginning my escape into my Maine summer days.

Billy goat

(Miami, 2022)

Billy goat skips on the rocks by the shore,
Fast bouncing, over and over.
He is out ahead, dodging the sea mist, as
they watch from a distance.

He never seems to tire.
Going, going, on his own, just out of reach.
He is young, and spry, and exploring free.
Small brown legs and bouncing brown hair,
As he leaps over gaps in the sea rocks,
past tide pools, and barnacle covered driftwood.

They let out a whistle and add in a hand wave for good measure.
It's almost time to go.
He hears their call and turns back.
Longing for more and just a few more turns along
the shore, as the sea and youth calls to him.
Alas,

His shoulders slump as he makes his way back toward them,
The car, the ride home, dinner and bed-time.
He will come back soon they promise.
And the sea and rocks will be waiting.

Billy Goat will run again, and skip and bounce as he always does,
Because it's in his bones and his heart,
And it will always be.

Thump, thump it goes

(Charleston, 2022)

Thump, thump went the sound on the pavement-cracked road,
My dead-end street haven (no traffic to interrupt me)
My afternoon escape ritual.

Freed from the walls of school and free for a while
from the parent's direction and the dinner bell,
My latch key existence.
I'd grab the worn orange ball and wear out the net
(so many times it was replaced with a chain),
The swish sound swallowed by the metal clink
In my mind I would pretend and imagine,
Keeping score of my games, picturing my favorite players,
Playing both fictitious teams, by myself
But never alone
My initials were carved in the cement base of the basketball hoop,
My claimed childhood court.

Thump, thump it went,
Over and over
Each afternoon day,
In the New England wind,
In the dusk light,
In the frozen afternoons,
In the sun swelter days.

These memories still held,
Fondness,
Free and simple,
Etched inside,
For always

57 Preston Place

(Charleston, 2022)

The old stone wall a continual work in progress
snaked around the edge of the estate
Keeping the pristine inside.

Arbor vitae stood tall and watched over the
gravel drive and the main door entrance.

An English gentleman gardener would plant the bulbs,
walk the box hedges,
And nip and tuck what was needed during his time back home.

The pond would call for ducks, then for
skates when it would freeze,
A perfect view from the kitchen window.

The enchanted pool nearly hidden from view
with the draping plants surrounding,
Keeping what's inside, inside
Including summertime dips and cold sparkling lemonade.

Honeysuckle, gardenia, and cottage pinks
would dance around the delphiniums,
Erect and striking in their purple shine,
Phlox and primrose around the edges,
And who could forget the roses?
Commanding glances from the birds and passersby.

Polly and Prue would bark and chase,
Jump after dragonflies and bees,
And greet me with their auburn and white
spaniel glory and mischief.

Another time was held on these grounds,
of proper and cultivated beauty,
made sharp with attention and dutiful
care (including mine).

I've grown older now, twenty years have lapsed
Since strong and brown,
I would mow and rake, and do my part to keep this tapestry alive.

A fond memory to revisit often,
I can nearly smell the scent of its summer air,
And long to sit again in the shade of the trees,
Content and free.

What could have been

(NYC, 2022)

I could have heard them chant my name,
As my hair flopped,
And I moved like lightning,
Cutting across the perfect green field,
Or,
Wandered beneath the ocean,
In my one-man submarine,
Looking out its glass window
To record important observations,
In a little official book,
To report back to the surface,
Or,
My boots could have been caked with thick mud,
Having trekked deeper in the jungle,
To understand the communal living of the last indigenous people,
Still as Rosseau described,
Primitive and noble,
Or,
Having finished the exam,
Tucked behind a dark wood desk,
With my books surrounding and my open green file folders,
Square leather briefcase in tow,
As I combed through matters of consequence,
ESQ Brice, in a small gold black on the shelf nearby,
Or,
With a mountain view, and perhaps a bearded face,
Writing my thoughts and reflections, in my black ink
In my colored notebooks,

Putting the words together just so,
On my own time, and translating to the waiting
Eyes and hearts
But instead, I sit,
Having lived a different set of lives than the ones once imagined,
Not quite still able to put a finger on,
What it is,
I am called,
Or known by,
But,
I can still kick the ball,
Dream of under the sea,
Have the call of the native in me,
And the allure of aristocratic tidy thinking,
And finally, now,
Begin to write it down,
In a way that is real for me,
Captures what could have been,
And perhaps,
Pieces of what it's all become.

Girls

(Plum Island, 2015)

I like the poems about girls,

even the ones that don't know it,

small details observed and captured
Like crooked fingers,

by a hoping, waiting, eye,

the ones that talk of shapes,
and scents that carry memories and make
dreams,
and capture just the right person in just the right way,

because they are part of her,

seen fully through drunken eyes.

The ones about her slipping away,

in the longing, pining, afterwards,

sometimes the truest thoughts revealed.

And when a pen is used like a flashing light

to daze and remind or to call out,

in an attempt to win again,
or maybe for the first time,

I like the poems of waiting, seeking, hoping hearts,

laid out for all to see.

Walking to school as a boy in a small town

(Charleston, 2022)

Out the door and down the slope of the
cracked asphalt till I hit the road,
The straps of my red Jansport pack on each shoulder.
I don't have a watch, but have rehearsed the
time it takes each day back and forth
I head up the Lyndsey's driveway, they are old and always home.
She watches from the kitchen window as I cut footprints
in the grass and pass the shed and into the woods.
Crunch goes the leaves,
The path is worn,
Three minutes and I am climbing the hill to Phil's house.
I step over a wiffle ball in the grass, left
over from our homerun derby.
Up the drive,
He isn't home,
And his dad has left.
Someday his sister will remind me of his mom.
I make quick work of Larch Row,
And I am in the front yard of the house with the swing set,
whose name we never knew. They never make a peep.
My eyes are on the fence ahead with the hole I climb through.
I'm in Toby and Wyatt's yard,
And the grass has been worn from our games of run-
down, and because Wayne is too busy for yard work.
There is a silver Peugeot in the driveway and
inside the empty yogurt container's MaryBeth
uses for cups, but embarrass the boys.

A brown pickup truck with the windows cracked
is parked crooked in the driveway,
Must have been another late night,
Maddie the strange bug-eyed terrier runs to the
door and warns everyone I am passing by,
Sometimes Wayne peers out and tells me the boys aren't ready,
Fine by me, my morning communion is always alone.
I'm at the edge of the driveway at the top of the hill and
I remember when I raced down in my vainglory on my
skateboard hoping Elizabeth would notice, but glad she
didn't when the speed was too much and I tumbled into
the ditch with a raspberry reminder, that stung more
when her dad called from the yard to ask if I was okay.
I turn left and pass the bigger houses that line the last stretch of
road before it dead ends in a circle and the woods reappear.
I step back into leaf dirt and it's 100 yards left till the
end with the old tan and green box waiting for me.
Sometimes the usual suspects are lounging on the trail for a
morning smoke, and I pick it up in my nose before I see them,
Lance against a tree in his motocross jacket and Josh who
all the girls now notice, three years my senior and no longer
inclined to acknowledge the eighth-grader lost in his thoughts.
I'm in the clear, and I come up to the side
door and climb three concrete steps,
And the double door is waiting.
18 minutes gone, I'll do it again tomorrow,
I grab the handle as the bell rings.

Chopping wood

(Charleston, 2022)

*From memory of L'abri, Greatham England 1998

I went to you in the morning,
across the gravel drive, and the horse stalls, now empty,
passing the raised garden, and leaving the
red brick of the manor house
behind,
into the English cold.

Tom from Minnesota with his greasy long hair,
Kind eyes, and lack of words was my companion.
He would crouch and work in the back of the
open shed, assembling in neat rows,
my finished work.

A block of fresh wood meat would be
placed on the large stump base,
and I would swing down with a rehearsed devastating split,
Splintering the wood, into neat pieces,

Whack, whack,

the axe my hammer I swung,
I would pull it back slow and full behind my ear,
My legs spread wide
and like a coil, I would plummet the head of
Iron down in a smooth arc.

I'd toss the piece aside, and watch him pick it up to stack,
and stack.
I never wore gloves, I liked the hardening
of callouses on my hands,
The full grip of the handle, the sweat grow over time in my palms.

We would stop for tea, in mid-morning, and
it was the first pause from the
rhythm, we created,

place, split, toss, stack,
place, split, toss, stack.

The pile grew thick and deep, and orderly,
Tom never grumbled, never questioned,
He in his own quiet world, cramming it higher and higher.

Two more hours, till lunch, and when I would finally acknowledge
the way my muscles felt, and survey the progress.

I had youth on my side, and it didn't feel like work,
I had my wandering thoughts, and the simple focus of providing
for the big hearth fire in the house, we would burn each evening.
Chop, chop, whack.
Chop, chop, whack.

In the rain days we would shell up in coats, and knee boots.
When it warmed, we would shed flannel shirts for, cotton,
and take our flat hats off so our hair could breathe.

Our station was strewn with towels, and tools,
Empty jugs of water, and footprints from
moving through the mud.

My back grew thick and my arms tighter,
I could hit the perfect spot and miss the knots
on the wood, by repetition's memory,
Hours would glide by.

August moved to November, and my daily chore continued,
out in the morning, back at lunch,
Tom and I in our shared duties,
the axe man, and the stacker.
the wood pile grew,
And all was as it should be.

Imprints

Moments become memories become me.

For Grandpa George

(Charlotte, close to Thanksgiving, 2017)

I'm not the only one who couldn't help
but smile when the mail arrived,
Seeing the familiar address from the middle
of America, the center of your world
A not yet forgotten time and place, preserved by you.

And to picture you sitting at the small
typewriter in the basement office
creating your living connections with those you care for,
Simply profound words of wisdom, humor and
gratefulness for all the small things in Life,

       A cup of fifty-cent coffee with friends,
       A weather report on grandma's tomatoes
       A legion newsletter heralding heroes that
       are still standing in quiet communion

I'll always remember the feel of your
hand, even stronger than mine,
Forged by years of work, that most only
have read about, but never done.

       early mornings, routine duties,
       planting seed,
       sowing rows,
       collecting eggs,
       governed by the movement of the sun and rains

Remembering the twinkle in your eye, born of a life fully lived,
In honesty,
family,
service
and meaning,

What imprints you have left, through each passing smile,
kindness unseen,
Food on the table for those you love,
and those you will never meet.

The years are catching up, and come for us all—
The broad shoulders, more rolled
the naps in mid-day easier to come by,
Like a quick thief,
the toil of labor and shoveling your own snow,
More evident in lines and wrinkles now.

And yet still you rise, and greet those in your large
world as if they are the only ones that matter.
While you still spread
your farmer's charm freely,

with ripples of blessing circling wide from each
act of connecting with those counted fortunate to know you.

As the good seed planted grows, and
provides for those that consume it
So, did you, more than perhaps you know

Take this as a small reminder,
and a token of thanksgiving.

Oliver

(Plum Island, 2013)

You grew on me quickly,
and I wasn't planning on enjoying you.

Assuming, huss, fuss and all the rest,
but you slipped in quietly and sure.

Effortlessly becoming a welcomed face,
whiskers and all.

Mostly you glided almost noiselessly,
from place to place,
maybe deliberately,
just how and when you were needed.

Softly seeking, exploring.
white patter paws, your small prrr,
given when you decided,
ball curled up in the sun,
with your old man gaze,
watching,
exhuming calm and confidence that
rubbed off, as steady and cool,
with a tail twitch here and there, to keep
me honest, and remind me,
my orange tabby friend.
I'll miss you dearly.

Basquiat

(New York, 2019)

"Every Single Line Means Something"
—Jean Michel Basquiat

Explosion in a concrete jungle,
your insides graffitied in raw defiance,
capturing realness in bursts, provocation and color.

Skulls, crowns, a dinosaur,
Jackie Robinson, black and white,
good and evil, and everything in between,
primitive and elegant,
and undeniable.

Truth and colors,
in words and pictures,
what others saw, but couldn't say,
modern slaves, power,
thirst, inner workings
jazz in motion,

You were lightning that hit between the eyes,
too bright for even yourself,
youth in all its wildness.

Several lifetimes crammed into twenty-seven years,
we can't forget, we won't.

As real today as it was then,
Flesh and spirit, and thirty million
Reasons why.
Thank you,

SAMO.

St. Paul's bells

(London, 2016)

All a chorus surrounding cacophony,
ringing,
dinging,
loud and full,
inescapable.

You can't keep a private thought as they tell
you it's time to listen and surrender.

It goes on, and builds like a stomping clamor,
In rhythm.

It's not gentle,
but it is beautiful,
and strong and full and ancient.

Each time, like the time before,
It cuts whatever is in its way, and heels it down.

How many ears have kneeled to this mighty sound?
Over years and years and still today,

Hearts reminded of glory and might,
And angels.

And that there is bigger stuff that's going on,
whether you like it, or even think about it,
(Although you should do both),

Mighty and grand,
the daily toll,
caught, me on the way to my afternoon meeting,

those bells.

Making plans

(Wenham, 2014)

He would always begin the show,
that same ritual,
hot liquids poured into blue and white cups,
cold milk and sugar cubes,
A tea cozy made of a knit chicken to keep it warm,
occasionally some of Penny's
homemade brown bread, and hard butter to
pat on with a flat blade.

We would sit across from each other,
stacked papers in between
the cat flickering a glance and a tail twitch,
the clock would slow down,
we were lost in re-fills,
and our thoughts,
and surrounded by the ever-growing garden,
we moved from subject to idea in our own meandering way,
between memories and plans,

Of how to unpack an artist's place in the world,
As he ages, and a young dreamer's
direction, as he too ages, and moves from yard helper,
to someone who speaks the strange language of selling
sacred paintings, sculptures and making known to many
the hidden treasures, collecting dust in the barn.

A revolving door of sideways progress,
interrupted by the cups getting dry,
crumbs on the plate, and our excuses of
moving on to the rest of the day.

Distracted by the inevitable,
days and weeks would go by,
and we would return,
to once again unfurl
our holy banter of the hearts.

Painting of a boat on the waves

(Amesbury, 2014)

I saw a painting once by an artist with a hard life, it was
large and deep and filled with waves all around.
A tiny boat with a white sail was drifting among
dark green and blue heavy paint,
like Homer but more fury.
But that boat wasn't done, although it probably should have been,
It had hope, and fight and spirit and
Light from the sky cut over the water.
And the artist wondered why no one had
bought the magnificent work
($4600) dollars' worth,
full of his story, and the realness of life,

But if they had, I wouldn't have seen it that day, hanging
boldly on the hallway brick of the converted mill studio,
And listened to it speak,
And it said, "the waves wont swallow that boat,
Not today."
Not this one,

And maybe that artist will never know that story,
And how many times he has shared, with many passing
by, and reminded them what they needed to hear,

As he stares up at the unsold painting,
And maybe that is how it sometimes goes.

For Seamus

(Charleston, 2022)

You were Ireland in all its mystery, suffering, glory and beauty.

The land in your parchment,
tales and stories in your pen,

A bard's song woven with stone, sea, dirt, and sky,
You spoke of blackberries, bogs,
Growing old, and being young.

I recognized myself in you,
In love with the land,
coming to grips with history,
Finding your way through careful observation,
Seeking, as you make your name and way,
Digging all the while.

While I've got no spade to follow a man like you,
You planted seeds twenty years ago,
When I first read your pages, and they've been
growing in their own time, ever since.

Now,
I'll sink my impulse like a bolt,
And not waiver.

A woman and her dog in snowy Chicago

(Charleston, 2021)

A woman and her dog in snowy Chicago went for a morning walk,
like the day before,
and the day that would come again.

The clockwork ritual of coats and gloves,
A leash, a coax,
A pat, a tug and a pull,
their morning dance.

They pattered through the hall, still quiet,
to the elevator, down they went
with morning pant sounds meeting morning
daytime thoughts warming up,

stepping out into the still dark air
city sounds purred awake,
and they moved in common rhythm into the new day air.

She led her on with intent and sometimes mischief,
smelling, seeing,
hurrying through the streets dotted with early
morning drivers, as they head to the lake path.

Together always they talk in a language just for
them, exchanging inside jokes, affections,
and questions to each other on what lies ahead.

Sometimes the dog tangos with other ones like her, or
growls away the ones she senses aren't quite right,
same with the people,
always thinking of the woman,
keeping her eyes and ears alert,
protecting,
keeping her to her.

Soon their feet leave the pavement and crunch into a snow
layer of dirt as the lake wind beckons and hits their faces.

She sticks out her tongue to taste the wind,
feeling more alive as the naturescape sweeps away the city bustle,

farther they go,
hand-in-paw,
In synchronized familiar step pattern,
under a sky starting to warm with daytime color.

Crunch, crunch goes the sound until they
find their chosen spot to sit,
the dog curls into a lazy ball to gaze at that lakeshore picture,
the woman tucks in her knees,
shoots out a firm breath,
and stares out into the day ahead.

After just the right amount of soaking time,
the woman calls out to the dog who knows
the drill and stands to attention,
reversing steps,
down the path, with birds now up and
people caught up to their early rise,
the lake world blends back to city life.

Over the sidewalks,
past the doormen,
their pace starts to quicken as the day comes into focus.

In the still cold, underfoot snow
minutes have turned into hours,
they stop at the familiar but inevitable building entrance,
the symbol reminder that the journey is almost at its end.

And the dog life and the woman in Chicago life
awaits them, even if they don't want it to,
when they reach the elevator,
the dog shoots a longing look of saucer brown eye pleas,
hoping to break the will of the woman for just a bit longer.

The woman answers back,
with her own soft brown eyes filled with a language beyond words,
and reminds her they still have the
evening walk to look forward to.

Eulogy

(Charlotte, 2016)

When it was done and gone it was,

but before it was,

eyes watched, un-movement

stilled and solemn

words spoken in remembrance
the wooden box holding,

crank and lowered down
ground to ground

small stone and soil,
all in all, all
that's ever left, ever said, or even done, undone,
not done, or almost done,

sealed and closed
and closed this chapter, story part,

just those moments,
last ones,

memories still bright
and in time,

many days will pass
with fewer thoughts and some flowers

then,

what's done is done,
and gone

For Paul Klee

(Boston, 2015)

Shapes placed just right,
in wonderful and wild order,
musical color with movement,
birds, a gold fish, and
buildings floating over the Tunisian sea,
primitive gentle meanings, inescapable.

The Zentrum halls left their indelible mark,
from that point onwards,
a kindred connection,
each time I saw you I dreamt a bit more,
and immediately spoke your language,

even though we never even met,
You will always be my favorite.

Max, while I write

(Charleston, 2022)

He sits lion majestic in a bed of leaves,
pink-black nose twitching around with the scents in the wind.

A blanket of cream white fluff,
and his eyes closed.

He wears the blue and orange handkerchief
dutifully around his thick neck.

Moving here and again to lick,
adjust his slumped stance,
and turn his head to gaze around the woods.

I watch him lay his head flat,
ears tucked back,
with his peacock tail at rest,
curled across his bear paw feet,

His breaths go in and out, making a rhythmic sound, Steady.

I shift my weight, lost in distraction and he
tilts up, aware of me, and I meet his
brown saucer eyes.

It's just a glance, but just what is needed,
I'll sit awhile longer,
He rolls on his back, feet stretched to the sky.

Sundays with Grandma

(Charleston, 2020)

You could smell the roast as you walked through the door,
mixing with the rich scent of potatoes, casseroles, and fresh rolls.

As you entered, all was neat, arranged, and carefully prepared.
A perfectly laid table, ornamental and welcoming.

Each time a ritual of familiarity would begin,
chairs brought in, as family gathered together.

All the while, a waif-like figure was moving
with intention and purpose,
pausing only to dart her crystal blue eyes to her subjects,
and send small orders for help and instructions,
everything moving according to plan.
Bent over sinks and counters, steadily pivoting
between hot dishes, plates and serving spoons, she
would survey her feast coming into focus.

You would hear a distinct laugh
In between her dance and small movements,
a mind that was sharp had caught a story or
comment from one of her loved ones,
that had allowed her to briefly embrace a
small moment for her,
of enjoyment.

At some point, the order would come that
it was time to come to the table.
As people shuffled to seats, they were greeted by
perfectly laid silverware, crisp napkins, shining plates,
and an orderliness that let one embrace their only task;
To eat, drink, be present together, and enjoy;
all had been planned and provided.

Hands were joined around the long table, and
grace was said for bounty and family.

An exquisite array of familiar trappings arrived,
bellies were filled and re-filled.

I would often eat as much as I could, just as
a way to show my thanks for the
hours of preparation, and to send a small token back to our
matriarch host (and I suspect I wasn't the only one guilty of that),

As family sat, stories and events caught up,
a bird-like figure, dressed neatly,
would interject careful comments,
grace us with more laughter,
and portray through her eyes,
that this event, this gathering,
brought her a special joy.

Plates were cleared away, and re-placed,
and the smell of rich coffee seeped into the room.

A second act, prolonging the togetherness,
sweets, brought in with small hands, and a twinkle.

After not an empty inch remained in bellies, another ritual began:
Of clearing and cleaning.

Each time someone would help, or a few,
but under the guise and direction of our culinary general.

In a seeming flash
all was put away, and back to a pristine state,

Next, retiring to the living room
to sit in comfy seats, and plush carpet,
all was as should be,
careful and welcoming

After hours of togetherness
creating memories and
bonding a close family, even closer,
It would become time to say goodbye.

Each person, would need to stoop down to embrace
her, and carry with them a token of her love

Until the next Sunday dinner arrived.

Nature's Calling

"The Lord God took the man and put him in the Garden
of Eden to work it and take care of it." (Genesis 2:15)

I have always felt most at peace, alive and
free by the sea, mountains and fields.

Appleton Farms

(Ipswich, 2014)

You had postcard beauty,
rolling hills meeting trees on the horizon,
crooked fences stretched across
to keep the wandering cows at bay.

I skied you in the winter,
crisscrossing and making my fresh-marked trails.

I remember the sound,

Chickadee and titmouse watched curiously
from the leafless branches,
under the grey-blue sky,
it was the quiet season.

In early spring, the in-between time,
I would walk your cool mornings,
and run your trails in the warming afternoons,
watching the buds creep, and colors shift toward new.

In the heat of summer your grass was thick,
Your sounds alive the most,
laughing and chatter of the families,
heading into the red open barn to collect
brown bags of yellow squash, bulging tomatoes
and slender beans, and carrots with bushy heads.

You showed fullest in fall,
as much of small-town New England does,
perfect sweater days, all the colors on display,
rust and dark yellows everywhere,
the softness of the leaves underfoot.

I met you often, during my own seasons,
visiting you as needed,
bringing guests,
adding to your living history,
creating moments now woven
into your ground
for always.

Beach in Tulum

(Tulum, 2017)

Sea sounds mix with wind turn to whirl,
rocking greetings—
steady, strong, rolling.

White clouds drift on blue field—spread above,
watching,

humming, splinter patterns
staccato, crescendo.

Green catches light,
swallows sand away
breaking time

this cool late day picture.

Sanderlings

(Sullivans Island, 2022)

Wiper blade feet scoot across the brown sand,
peck, peck, quick,
beak reaches down
head bobbing,
eyes dart,
seeking.

Around the sea grass piles,
outrunning the tide,
fast and sure,
your focused pursuit.

Scurry, scurry, pause

I sit in my slowest state for days with the sun on my chest,
you pass by with intent as if I wasn't there,
Racing on for your morning meal.

After the storm

(Charleston, 2022)

Wet mud and crooked trees,
the air is cool,

grey clouds still skating by,
the sun is hiding.

The leaf floor is cluttered with branches,
As the bird songs inch back in,

drops of old rain fall from above
Making a sound, when the wind blows.

Last night all was shaken,
It felt it would never end,

In this morning,
the world seems cleaner now.

Sunset drive

(Plum Island, 2016)

It crept and slipped down,

like it always does,

and yet never the same way,

this time an even more gloaming, tempered
fade, as if holding on for a bit more.

Silver pulls on rose, grabs the grey-blue
tails and rests over the hills.

a wide smile,

a contented comfort,

a mirror for any looking now.

Soon the sister with dark fingers will appear,

but for now the light still lingers,

sweetly.

Ducks on the water

(Amesbury, 2016)

Quack, glide, swoosh

quack, glide, swoosh

glide, sliding by

eddy, ripple, move

eddy, ripples, mov(ed)

quick, splash, woosh
quick, splashing, woosh

settle down smooth
settle down smooths

glide, smooth, move

Sand crabs

(Costa Rica, 2017)

Scurrying on tiny legs,
moving intently across the sand
Slow, sometime quick
You can curl up in a moment.
Then peeking,
back again, and off
noiselessly.
Sideways and forwards,
Where are you going, so surely?
Always off again,
hurriedly,
Some big,
others small
Each with your covering and your claws,
What a wonder to behold.

At the shore without cares

(Jamaica, 2016)

Sun on the waves like a blanket
rolling in, rolling over
this light sparkle beaming.
Hush goes the sound,
over and over,
in its washing trance, through a small breeze.

Cool mixed with warmth,
salt smells,
palms move,
laps on the sand.

Color words

(Beverly Farms, 2002)

Bluesy
Whiter
Greyest
Oranged
Pinkly
Greening

Living canvas

(Wenham, 2015)

I got lost in its wild wonder,
a sprawling growing mass,
as diverse, and intricate as its creator,
with small curated details hidden among
Its explosion of life.

From the back of the barn steps,
around the old fence and the
formal box hedge garden,
through the paths
cut and laid over the creek,
down to the lake shore,
where the blue canoe rested.

The tennis court where Anne ran pico through jumps,
now a mossy patch of wildflowers,
surrounded by ferns, and day lilies.

The big pine, like an out-of-place statue,
created a shade to sit.

The bird (or was it a chili pepper?), cutting over
the grass, you couldn't look past it.

The wire of the old chicken coop, attached
to the lower barn still stood,
rusty and hex shaped.

And the stone walkway weaved to the
upper lot, where moss mingled with wildflowers
and an assortment of bird feeders hung overhead,
from birch branches and maples.

It had trails and tucked corners,
and piles of dirt,
mulch, transplanted shrubs in constant rotation,
shovels, barrels to catch the rain,
and stakes to help the young plants grow straight.

This wasn't a yard, or a garden, anymore,
but a place,
to walk and study,
and to work,
like he did, early in the morning, till the
bugs came out at dusk, and it grew too dark to
see.

It was the artist's new canvas,
playful,
expressive, and a work in constant progress,
never quite finished, but filled with
expression,
like each of us.

A windy day haiku

(Charlotte, 2018)

Chimes whistle their song,

Leaves dance wild in the day wind,

Swaying thoughts abound.

Later On

"When I became a man, I put away childish things, including the fear of childishness and the desire to be very grown up."
—C.S Lewis

"Without transition, a change is just a rearrangement of the furniture."
—Williams Bridges

Birds and worry

(Charleston, 2022)

Look at the birds of the air,

(I do and see freedom up above)

They do not sow or reap, or store away in barns,

(But they have wings, and I don't)

Are you not much more valuable than they?

(One would hope, but it may depend on who you asked)

Can any of you by worry add a single hour to your life?

(You got me with that one)

Time

(Newburyport, 2014)

You are a thief,
gone each moment,

Sometimes you stretch and hold
At your discretion,

Or freeze in place, just for a while,
and live in memories and pictures,

But always moving,
At your pace,

Unstoppable,
despite my best efforts.

The old saw

(Charleston, 2022)

Thumb on the choke,
prime ten times,
grab the t-bar,
yank hard,
a rattle sound spurts,

Again.

Pull the cord back high,
release the hand brake,
humming, humming,
almost catches,
then
stops,

I loosen the blade, fingers on the chain,
making sure they are snug in its track,
tighten up with the ratchet,
screw down clockwise,
back to the beginning,

Choke, prime, pull,
rattle,
hum, hum,
prrr,
stop.

I have wood to cut quickly.
The motor tool does all the work,
neat,
fast,
slice,
hurry along.

Now what?

damn power tools.

I see the orange handle of the old boy in the corner of the garage,
rusty curved blade and all,
last ceremoniously used for the Christmas tree,

He doesn't have it in him,
nor I the time.

It's a crisp fall afternoon, with birds and the kids are at bay,
and the queen is occupied.

I grab him by the hand and walk down the long driveway to
the pile sitting cross legged from the storm weeks ago,

I bend down and the teeth bite,
And I pull, elbow to the sky,
I see the dust appear and I hear the pure sound,
not the buzzing hum of speed and efficiency,
this is the sound of
repetition, focus,
And slow strength,

I am twenty-three again with brown arms and sweat.
time drifts by, as the first one splits.

I think briefly, this will take all day.
then I cut again,
another falls,
and I toss my progress toward the pavement,

I am happy and free,
I like the soft sound,
and even the time it takes,

The pile gets bigger,
I remember who I am,

The old saw in hand.

Jug (GW given by GD)

(Charleston, 2022)

You came as a present on a special day,
Which I have to remember,
From at the time, my closest friend,
Since gone,
And I didn't realize your significance,
Then,
But I do now.

You were actually my first one,
Black, grey, white, and in-between,
Shades, texture,
haunting,
An everyday item from yesteryears,
In your simple black metal rectangular wrapping,
placed perfectly,
The paper has faded to a pinkish hue,
Against the still white mat,
twenty-one years later.

Over the years, and my seasons
you have travelled with me,
downstairs in the Essex hallway,
up to the Salem attic room,
the living room corner in the small blue house close to the sea,
then to the country and green saltbox,
A stop on the island, overlooking the marsh,
to the in-between place, upstairs while I worked,
landing in the big southern brick estate,

Displayed in the large open room, looking to the woods,
finding your way to the small cul de sac,
In the corridor, so I could see you,
now to the open woods great room,
first thing by the door.

From North to South,
close to the ocean, and in the woods,
on car streets, and in the open,
and through all that, you've stayed the same,
your stillness and brush stroke movement,
the pencil signature of the artist,
who showed me what it meant to be free,
and to look carefully and to create.

I keep moving you with me,
through each season, steady reminders
of the deep, all that's changed,
and the parts that are still the same.

Succulents

(Plum Island, 2014)

They don't need much,

a nice spot to catch the sun, and maybe show off a bit,

but you can't forget 'em.

or you'll pay for it.

They will let you know in their own way,

even without words.

Dry up, fall off, wither some.

even rot out,

If you're really careless.

Don't forget,

just a smattering of liquid.

it's important.

(an ice cube can be perfect; slow melt and feeding),

and boy will they love you,

and be happy.

Just a bit of care.

A nice spot, and they can sit and watch it all.

and can be there for a long time.

you can even name them.

They won't mind.

Growing up

(Tulum, 2017)

Days slipped into years quick and quietly.
staring back to remind me.
From that first lightning bolt jolt within
blue pools arresting,
to those deeper hues now soaked in life
and memories, bedtime stories,
and now,
longer limbs and more choices,
independence and pages turning,
a longing wish still cradled in my arms,
with sweet rhythm breath, and no cares,
only sleeping.
We move together now,
discovering each other in new ways,
new steps to take, some closer, others away,
learning as we go, looking back at times,
but forever holding.

Mowing the grass

(Charlotte, 2017)

I step outside,
the perfect break,
feet in front of feet,
having my straight rows
a hum motor sound,
just the speed to increase
catching my thoughts.

Smells of cut green,
a trickle of sweat
each pass is progress,
this small stroke of artistry,
a recurring tradition.

The week begins again soon,
the lawn's fresh face is ready,
and grinning thanks.

Starting over

(Charleston, 2021)

Begin again,
sit back down
you've been here before.

The start really matters.

Like the rock down the hill,
rolling up steam and movement,
laying its path
carrying on once it gets rolling.

So, get in the seat.
the paper won't bite,
the pen may bleed,
the thoughts may hide,
but maybe they'll just jump out with a scream,
And say "thank you."

Pulling weeds

(Asheville, 2021)

Bent down on my knees and searching,
for just the place to grab,
closest to the root (you have to get the whole thing).

It's a sun-caked afternoon,
and they are everywhere, polluting the
thick green lawn,
different lengths and patterns,
provoking, teasing in their defiance,
speckling the would-be even greenery.

My eyes lock in, and I'm in action,
feeling the resistance, I tear with precision,
and make small piles to collect later on.

The pace is slow,
sweat beads on my neck, and under my arms,
my thoughts drift, but never too far from the next target.

Pluck, pull, look, move, inch,
the victims brown in the heat, no longer tied to
the earth, no longer mingling where they shouldn't be.

My fingers dig into the earth,
It getting clearer and I can't remember
how long I've been working.

I stand up, and my back is tight,
I survey the progress,
and make a note to stop waiting so long to pull the weeds.

She wanted a goat

(Newburyport, 2013)

She always wanted a goat,

even though she had one already.

What she REALLY wanted,

was one that didn't talk much,

and ALWAYS,

wanted to be

petted.

Photograph

(Charleston, 2022)

Their sepia-toned faces peer over at me,
keeping watch.

They are frozen in youth,
and their best attire,
A pinstripe suit, tie and white collar,
and she in her black low-neck dress,
with dark lips and full eyebrows.

I have his eyes,
The woman is striking and cold,
old time beauty with class,
you can't look away, but you can't look too long.

I have the shape of her face,
maybe her aloofness as well,

she passed her beauty down to her daughter,
but not the iron resolve.

His look is filled with dreams and some disappointments,
baby-faced, with a wry grin,
and perfectly placed hair.

This picture is before he discovered his genius,
and before his weaknesses took over.

When they were just starting out,
with plans,
before adding two more,
before all that followed.

I never met him, but they say
I resemble him, and I can see it,

I met her, and remember the
burning blue of her eyes.

They sit in silence, looking out across the room.
Every now and then, I look back,
And wonder.

Deepest Affection

"Four times my heart has doubled in size, each a marvel and the object of my deepest affection."
—Juntos nosotros, Mi Amore

Packed clothes

(Plum Island, 2014)

Small tender hands

folding carefully,

neatly,
gently placing each,

in ordered sequence.

Tucking right and perfectly,

a reminding testament,

this small act of a patient love,

displayed yet again.

Fairy houses

(Charleston, 2022)

The cooling air of an October afternoon wrapped around us,
acorns, red berries, splinters of twig, our hunted treasure.

A small warm hand my companion,
life was everywhere,

We crunched through leaves and over branches until we
found the bottom of the trees with the secret holes inside.

The sun shone on our skin,
her questions flowed freely with her small voice,

What food do they like?
Do they need a place to sit?
What color are their wings?

And our imagination wove together, as we
collected and assembled three houses with
our focused care, for our tiny friends.

Her blue eyes shone bright with wonder,
her skin, rose and sweat soft from our work.

We spied from the edge of the grass to see if they would come.

Then laid side by side,
staring at the trees and blue sky,
as I froze this memory,
to stay with me always.

Two tigers

(Plum Island, 2015)

Two tigers tussled for the night,

leapt and struck fiercely on each other,

paws pawing paws,

fur ruffled with playful fervor abandoned,

as only they can and do.

And what a sound and sight,

one on top of the other,

only long enough to be rolled back and

stare up at strong eyes, and pointing ears.

Round and round they went,

stripes blending into a blanket,

then lying still and solemn,
proud,

---

as only they can and do.

Tails flicking back and forth,

that hypnotic swooshing motion,

(purrrinnggg).

Ollie

(Beverly, 2006)

It came out,

a shudder, a shiver,
electric,

a thousand, million, hundred questions,
a million, thousand, hundred thoughts.

Scream,
you sweetest noise.

My arms felt floating.

Eyes like tiny black pearls, deep
soft, new.

Time raced frozen by.

It will never be the same,
I could feel warmth, I had never known

hello,
and forever.

Jack

(Charleston, 2022)

I remember how it felt to lift your small warm body,
even then thick and full,
up high in my arms.

Your white-blonde hair matted to your forehead,
your wide grin,
full cheeks,
and grey-blue soft eyes staring up at me.

I've watched the years pass and your limbs
are now long(er) than mine.

Shoulders broadening,
hair darkening,
eyes bright but older with
things seen.

You're quieter now, with your own thoughts and plans,
But when you walk, I notice my movement,
And we toss the football, and I never want it to end,
Because I know it will one day.

Your voice is deeper, and your time your own.
Your wide grin isn't given away so freely anymore,
But when you let it out, I see you up to my knee reaching up
with your hands to be carried around, in your proud perch,
and I hear the sound of your once small voice again,
"da da"
The sweetest sound.

Isla

(Charleston, 2022)

Shot from a cannon you land with the patter clap of your tiny feet,
moving as if they are too fast to touch the floor.

Around the corner you appear,
bouncy mane of chestnut curls upon curls,
smile wide and bright,
And those eyes...
electric dark and the biggest blue.

Subduing me on contact, bending me to your will,
you are unbridled energy,
a whirl of impulse and purpose.

I've never seen joy incarnate quite like you,
contagiously you catch those around you
In your net of excitement (and I am a happy prisoner).

Words tumble out, commands and desires
wrapped as one, as you bound closer towards me,
magnetic in your pull, I can't possibly resist.

And in that same flash, you're off,
to your next conquest, or perhaps a snack,
or a few toys to toss around for a bit,
but whatever awaits next,
is no match for you.

Maeve

(Charleston, 2022)

I guess we should have known when we named you,
"The intoxicating one / she who rules,"
just didn't expect it would only take a look.

With those almond eyes that change colors,
Green,
then bluish,
to speckle,
And back again,
but always steady, searching,
and connecting.

You are the youngest, smallest one,
with your tiny hands, and moving faster now to keep up,
exploring and discovery all around,
making your cooing sounds and your
easy laugh.

I love to see your wisps of reddish hair,
looking at the door
with your nose pressed to the glass,
and watch your hands stretch up when
I walk in.

I'm older now,
fourteen years between,
in a new season,
but kept young
with a full heart,
when I think of you,
now, and for always.

Mi Esposa

(Charlotte, 2018)

A smile from within,
with a tender touch, and strength,
eyes that dance and wait patiently.
A heart that beats in my rhythm,
opened wide and rooted in memories,
like a spring flowing and covering.

Her hands are small and wrapped around me
I'll keep them always.

Waves in my ocean,
I love the sound.

Fly

(Plum Island, 2014)

Fly
tiny white bird
your wings are strong
you have them
stretch

Fly
Over the sun

Kiss the sky
Kiss the clouds
Kiss the day

Fly away
From here
Over to tomorrow
It's there,
green and far
Your heart is gold

Fly
Tiny white bird

Eden

(Jamaica, 2017)

All melted away with each tide lapping the sand.
A big sky above,
painted clouds,
our browning happy bodies,
naked thoughts abound,
time is sleeping.
We drifted in the warm green blanket of the sea's embrace,
for a moment swallowed whole,
the loud reminder of what silence sounds like.
Breezes brushed by,
All in perfect harmony,
This forgotten life,
Full and calling
Our own Eden.

9 7 9 8 3 5 0 7 0 4 8 0 8